I0176938

Good Evening, Heavenly Father, How Was Your Day?

McDougal & Associates
Servants of Christ and Stewards of the Mysteries of God

Good Evening, Heavenly Father, How Was Your Day?

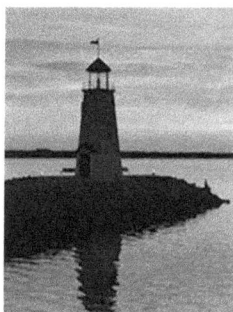

by

Linda Gourdine-Hunt

Unless otherwise noted, all Scripture references are from *The New King James Version of the Bible*, copyright © 1979, 1980, 1982, by Thomas Nelson, Inc., Nashville, Tennessee. References marked "KJV" are from the *King James Version of the Bible, public domain.* References marked "CEV" are from the *Holy Bible, Contemporary English Version,* copyright © 1995 by American Bible Society, New York, New York. References marked "AMPC" are from *The Amplified Bible, Classic Version,* copyright © 1954, 1958, 1962, 1964, 1965, 1987 by The Lockman Foundation, La Habra, California. References marked "RSV" are from *The Revised Standard Version of the Bible,* copyright © 1946, 1952, 1971, 1973 by the Division of Christian Education of the National Council of the Churches of Christ in the U.S.A. References marked "ESV" are from *The Holy Bible, English Standard Version,* copyright © 2001 by Crossway Bibles, a division of Good News Publishers. References marked "CEB" are from *The Common English Bible,* copyright © 2011 by Common English Bible, Nashville, Tennessee. References marked "NLT" are from *The New Living Translation of the Bible,* copyright © 1996 by Tyndale House Publishers, Inc., Wheaton, Illinois. References marked "NIV" are from the *Holy Bible, New International Version,* copyright © 1973, 1978, 1984 by International Bible Society, Colorado Springs, Colorado.

GOOD EVENING, HEAVENLY FATHER, HOW WAS YOUR DAY?
Copyright © 2016 — Linda Gourdine-Hunt
ALL RIGHTS RESERVED!

No part of this book may be reproduced or transmitted in any form or by any means, electronic or mechanical, including photocopying, recording, or by any information retrieval system.

Published by:

McDougal & Associates
18896 Greenwell Springs Road
Greenwell Springs, LA 70739
www.ThePublishedWord.com

McDougal & Associates is dedicated to the spreading of the Gospel of Jesus Christ to as many people as possible in the shortest time possible.

ISBN 978-1-940461-25-0

Printed on demand in the U.S., the U.K. and Australia
For Worldwide Distribution

Dedication

To my father, Nathaniel Gourdine,
who introduced me to the knowledge of God,
our heavenly Father
and who modeled the value of an excellent work ethic.

I can still hear him saying:

Christ is the Answer!
Rise and shine and give God the glory!
The early bird gets the worm.
Remember: God first, your dignity and then education.

Acknowledgments

God, for His message, vision and grace that enabled me to do this work for His glory.

Special thanks to my husband, for your loving support and encouragement throughout the long process of writing this book. You are the most patient person I know. You are such a blessing.

My heartfelt thanks to my aunt, Katherine McIver. Words cannot express how much I appreciate you. Your endless enthusiasm and invaluable expertise enhanced my ideas and greatly added to this project, especially your contribution to Chapter 6 "God's Work of Pouring Out His Love."

To my wonderful family and friends who supported me, thank you. I am deeply grateful for your love, prayers, energy and time. You helped to bring this book to completion and to make it a success.

Minister Sekou Laidlow, I will always remember our divine encounter at the library. Thank you for taking the time to share your expertise about writing the unemployment office scene in Chapter 3. It made a difference.

McDougal & Associates, my publishers, I am so grateful. Thank you.

Contents

*Oh that men would praise the L*ORD *for his goodness, and for his wonderful works to the children of men!*

Psalm 107:15 and 31, KJV

Tell of all his wondrous works!

Psalm 105:2, ESV

Introduction

It was an evening in March 2011, and I had just come in from work and slumped down in the love seat in the living room. "Whew! So glad I'm home sweet home again!"

Sliding down from the love seat, I stretched out on the furry rug in front of the fireplace and began thinking about the accomplishments that had come out of the challenges of my workday.

"Oh, Lord, I thank You," I silently prayed. "Couldn't have gotten through this day without Your help. Counseling young people in today's world is not possible in my own strength. They have so many needs. Lord, how I need You to tell me what to say and what to do. Help my students as they arrive on the grounds of the school every day."

It was then, while I was reflecting on the day's events, that the thought first surfaced, a thought I'd never had before and a question I had never asked before. If my day was like this, then what did God's day look like?

I immediately sat up, filled with curiosity and excitement. In awe of God, I looked up to Him and humbly uttered these words: "Good evening, heavenly Father, how was Your day?" That was the beginning of my quest, but I knew from the start that it was to be more than a personal curiosity. God had given me that thought because He wanted me to write a book on the subject. Allow me now to take you on my step-by-step quest to explore God's work in our lives.

As the days went on, I sought the Lord in prayer about writing the book. "What do You want me to say?" I asked. "I realize that I cannot write it from an intellectual perspective. I need You, Lord, to reveal to me something about Your day so that I will know what to say to others.

"What I can think about Your day is far too wonderful for me. I have to make myself stop thinking about it and change the subject. If not, it feels like my head might just burst. I cannot fathom all of the things You do in any one day. And You never slumber or sleep, as we do. You are always spreading Your love all over creation. Your words cannot be contained in books, so how do I present this for Your glory?"

The answers did not come immediately or all at one time, and I still am not satisfied that I have learned enough. There is so much more that I want to know. But slowly and surely the revelations began to come.

I must say up front that this book is in no way an exhaustive inventory of the innumerable things our heavenly Father does in our earthly understanding of twenty-four hours. Rather, it is a snapshot or a series of snapshots based on information derived from His Word, from nature, from media reports, from the personal testimonies of others, and from what He has revealed to me personally.

Introduction

In truth, no human mind could take in all that God does. He is lovingly and actively working to care for all of His creation every single day. This is beyond all human thinking and understanding. But He loves us so much that He does reveal much that we can understand. Come, journey with me into the heart of God, as we ask Him together, *"Good Evening, Heavenly Father, How Was Your Day?"*

Linda Gourdine-Hunt
Springfield Gardens, NY

DIVINE INSPIRATIONS
MESSENGER

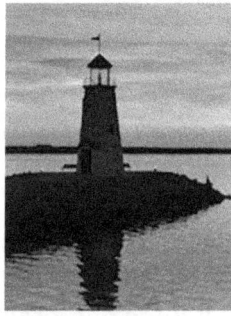

Chapter 1

God's Work of Creation

Early one morning I got up pondering the same question. During my prayer and meditation time, I was impressed by the Holy Spirit to read the story of Creation:

The First Day

He separated light from darkness and named the light "Day" and the darkness "Night. Evening came and then morning – that was the first day.

Genesis 1:4-5, CEV

The Second Day

God said, "I command a dome to separate the water above it from the water below it." And that's what happened. God made the dome and named it "Sky." Evening came and then morning – that was the second day. Genesis 1:6-8, CEV

The Third Day

God said, "I command the water under the sky to come together in one place, so there will be dry ground."

And that's what happened. God named the dry ground "Land," and he named the water "Ocean." God looked at what He had done and saw that it was good. God said, "I command the earth to produce all kinds of plants, including fruit trees and grain." And that's what happened. The earth produced all kinds of vegetation. God looked at what He had done, and it was good. Evening came and then morning – that was the third day.   Genesis 1:9-13, CEV

The Fourth Day

God said, "I command lights to appear in the sky and to separate day from night and to show the time for seasons, special days, and years. I command them to shine on the earth." And that's what happened. God made two powerful lights, the brighter one to rule the day and the other to rule the night. He also made the stars. Then God put these lights in the sky to shine on the earth, to rule day and night, and to separate light from darkness. God looked at what He had done, and it was good. Evening came and then morning – that was the fourth day.   Genesis 1:14-19, CEV

The Fifth Day

God said, "I command the ocean to be full of living creatures, and I command birds to fly above the earth." So God made the giant sea monsters and all the living creatures that swim in the ocean. He also made every

kind of bird. God looked at what He had done, and it was good. Then He gave the living creatures his blessing – He told the ocean creatures to live everywhere in the ocean and the birds to live everywhere on earth. Evening came and then morning – that was the fifth day.   Genesis 1:20-23, CEV

The Sixth Day

God said, "I command the earth to give life to all kinds of tame animals, wild animals, and reptiles." And that's what happened. God made every one of them. Then He looked at what He had done, and it was good.

God said, "Now we will make humans, and they will be like us. We will let them rule the fish, the birds, and all other living creatures." So God created humans to be like Himself; He made men and women. God gave them his blessing and said: "Have a lot of children! Fill the earth with people and bring it under your control. Rule over the fish in the ocean, the birds in the sky, and every animal on the earth.

I have provided all kinds of fruit and grain for you to eat. And I have given the green plants as food for everything else that breathes. These will be food for animals, both wild and tame, and for birds." God looked at what He had done. All of it was very good! Evening came and then morning — that was the sixth day.   Genesis 1:24-31, CEV

The seventh day, of course, was the day of rest. What an awesome God we serve!

When we look at the sixth day, we see that a big part of God's plan was for man to love Him and to take control of and manage His creation. To that end, God supplied man with everything he would need to live and grow in His love. God still provides for His children. During the course of every day, our Father is our Deliverer, Healer, Encourager, our All and All.

As I lay on my prayer rug after reading all of this, I said to myself, "Hmm, this day thing..." I could just imagine our heavenly Father still at work, looking over His great creation and saying:

- From My throne in glory, I surveyed the waters of the world and My creatures in the sea.
- At the Bronx Zoo, I took pleasure in seeing how My children were amazed and entertained by the animals and birds I created.
- I smiled as I heard Farmer Dolby in Wisconsin give Me thanks for the good crops of sweet corn and snap beans that he had planted.
- I stood on top of Mount Everest to view the hills and plains below.
- I stopped by the Veteran's Hospital in Texas to heal those soldiers returning from the war.
- I encouraged missionaries in India who are building a school for orphans with disabilities.

On June 17, 2012, when I asked, "Good evening, heavenly Father, how was Your day?" I added, "Happy Father's Day to You." Surely He deserves all of the honor, all the praise, and all the glory every single day because of who He is and what He does.

On March 15, 2012, I heard a message from a minister on television that answered some questions for me. He gave God's job description as follows:

- He directs our path.
- He unfolds and manifests the will of the Father to the Church.
- He brings us an expected end.
- He established many things for us before we were ever born.
- He guides us perpetually.
- He shows us great and mighty things.
- He calls us out and separates us for His work.
- He validates us.
- He will finish the work He has begun in us.

Yes, He does all that and so much more.

Oh that men would praise the L<small>ORD</small> for his goodness, and for his wonderful works to the children of men!

Psalm 107:15 and 31, KJV

Tell of all his wondrous works!

Psalm 105:2, ESV

CHAPTER 2

GOD'S WORK OF PROVIDING FOR EACH OF US

Therefore I tell you, do not worry about your life, what you will eat or drink; or about your body, what you will wear. Is not life more important than food, and the body more important than clothes? Look at the birds of the air; They do not sow, or reap, or store away in barns, and yet your heavenly Father feeds them. Are you not much more valuable than they?

Matthew 6:26-26, NIV

The Heavenly Father
The Heavenly Throne
YOUR PRAYERS

Yesterday, Today, and Forever

Dearly Beloved:

It gives Me the greatest pleasure to be your heavenly Father, Lord and Savior for your life. I am He who saves souls and meets all of your personal needs according to My riches in glory. I will never leave you or forsake you, and I am always on time.

I know that the combination of My unconditional love, wisdom and unmatched experience proves to be an eternal treasure to every person in relationship with Me. Please continue to reach out to Me with YOUR PRAYERS twenty-four hours a day, seven days a week, for I neither slumber nor sleep. I am waiting to hear from you, and I promise to answer your call.

With Loving-Kindness,
Your Heavenly Father

Waiting before our heavenly Father, Creator of the Universe, I could see Him in my mind's eye, smiling and saying, "Umm, 'Good evening, heavenly Father, how was Your day?' now that's a good question. I don't get that one very often." What followed were a few vivid snippets of situations and events that flooded my mind, almost as though I was watching a movie:

- Our Lord was helping Little Bo Peep find her lost sheep.
- A mother cried out to Him for her sick child, and He touched and healed the child's body.
- In the jungles of Africa, an elephant was stuck in the mud. The owner, a chieftain, needed him for transportation. God caused a caravan that was actually headed in the opposite direction to suddenly change course and help to free the elephant.
- Timmy was crying because he was struggling on a math test. He desperately needed to pass because he wanted his father to be proud of him. He bowed his head and whispered a prayer. Jesus heard that prayer. Timmy dried his tears and answered the questions, each one with the correct response.

I thought about my own daily life, all the things I ask the Lord for in a single day. Multiply that by the millions of people who love Him, and it becomes mind-boggling.

I arose, knowing that I wanted to learn more. I would make inquiry into a day with the heavenly Father. I wrote out and pinned a note to my bulletin board: TO BE CONTINUED.

Can we possibly imagine God's day? He keeps the stars and the moon in place, along with all of the planets. He is in charge of all the water everywhere. He guides planes through the vastness of space. And He cares for all of the innumerable animals alive today.

God commands the hills and mountains at will and causes the rain to fall. On top of that, He listens to all of our requests and supplies all of our needs. Wow! God is busy!

Regarding those requests, many times we cannot understand why God answers us the way He does. We can even feel confused and angry, because things don't go our way. But how could we possibly understand the mind of God? What we can know is that He loves us and works for our good. It is amazing enough just to know that He takes care of all the things He does. What an awesome God!

On the evening of August 8, 2012, I went to the Post Office in Rochdale Village, New York. On the way back I sat on a bench near the bus stop on the corner of Bedell Street and Baisley Avenue, exchanging an occasional conversation with an elderly woman. I also pondered again the question: *"Heavenly Father, how was Your day?"*

Suddenly, I heard in my mind's ear? "What day and where? A day globally? A day in New York State? A day in your community of Springfield Gardens? Or a day in your own personal life?"

Um, I hadn't thought about it like that. Our heavenly Father was busy. Volumes of books could never contain all that He does, but in my spirit I could hear:

- I walked alongside those who strolled in Central Park today.

- I soothed a soldier on the battlefield who was concerned about his wife and children back home.
- I comforted a prisoner in stocks who felt completely isolated.
- I gave dreams and visions to many of my children who are seeking answers to their prayers.

He continued: "I am in control. I am God. My day is full of love and compassion. It is full of hope and blessings. I look on My creation, all of it. I am God.

"My day is for My good pleasure. Sometimes I am disappointed, I am angered, I am sad because My children who are called by My name are not moving Me when they do not pray.

If my people who are called by my name, will humble themselves and pray and turn from their wicked ways, then I will hear from heaven, and I will forgive their sin and will heal their land. 2 Chronicles 7:14, NIV

"There is more that I want to do for you. There is more you are called to do. Come to Me, talk to Me, walk with Me, My child, and I will show you more good things in any given day."

... being confident of this, that he who began a good work in you will carry it on to completion until the day of Christ Jesus. Philippians 1:6 NIV

God is Truth. God is Love. He is the same yesterday, today and forever.

Chapter 3

God's Work of Hiring Laborers for His Harvest

As we labor for God's glory, our job description, according to Proverbs 3:5-6, is the following:

- **To trust in God with all of our heart**

- **To lean not to our own understanding**

- **To acknowledge Him in all our ways**

I could envision our heavenly Father rushing down to the nearest Unemployment Office early in the morning. There was a glowing smile on His face, and His eyes were beaming with excitement, in anticipation of those who are called by His name showing up in droves for guaranteed employment in His Kingdom. He positioned Himself in the middle of the room, where all who came in could see Him. He also conducted some interviews by phone.

The walls in the Unemployment Office were dark gray and Help Wanted ads were posted on them all around the room. The long lines wrapped around the hallways, and there were no more seats on the peeling brown wooden benches. There was standing room only, and people impatiently shifted from one foot to the other on the worn carpet. Some were murmuring, others were cursing, and one child was crying uncontrollably because she was hungry. A few staff members were drinking coffee and chitchatting about the game the night before.

A series of skits will serve to describe what takes place there:

THE RELUCTANT SERVANT

Heavenly Father: Welcome, daughter. Are you here to apply for service in My Kingdom?

Sister Carver: Oh yes, Lord, I want to serve You. Oh, yes!

Heavenly Father: Wonderful! I have an immediate opening for someone who will show My love to those who are homeless, those who are cold, hungry and dirty, who ...

Sister Carver: [Interrupting] Please excuse me, Lord. As You can see on my resume, I have not one and not two, but three degrees in Human Relations. I have served on the Leadership Society Board, I am well known and established in the community and have been a member of the church for thirty years now. [Pauses] And I give lots of money to the church. I know that I am well qualified for the position of ... [walking over to the wall, she points] President of the ...

Heavenly Father: Daughter, are you here to serve in My Kingdom or not?

Sister Carver: Yes, Lord, but not in the way You suggest. "Cold, hungry and dirty ..." ? No, I want to be President of the ...

Heavenly Father: [Not allowing her to finish] Daughter, I love you. Call Me when you really want to follow Me and do it My way. [With this, He turns away from her and calls to the line,] Next!

The Watchful Witness

Heavenly Father: Welcome, My son. Are you here to serve in My Kingdom?

Jaquan: Yes, Lord. I would be so honored to serve You ... that is, if You can use someone like me.

Heavenly Father: What do you mean?

Jaquan: Well, God, I done a lot of bad things in my life. As a matter of fact, I'm amazed that I'm even alive today. I wasted seventeen years of my life in jail. I don't have a lot of education, I don't have a legal resume, and I don't have any money. But I want to do something, whatever You say, because I asked You to forgive me and You did. I know that You love me. You have proven it to me over and over again. To show my love in return, is there anything that I can do to serve?

Heavenly Father: Yes, son, there is. Be a witness to others about My grace, mercy and everlasting love. Tell them about My willingness and power to forgive them and bless them, as I have blessed you.

Jaquan: [Falling down at the Lord's feet] Oh, thank You, God, but I'm not sure I'm suited for that. Sometimes my words ... my words don't come out right.

Heavenly Father: Just obey Me. The Holy Spirit will help you in your time of need. I love you. Go, now, and spread My love. [They embrace and Jaquan departs.]

The Emboldened Encourager

(A Telephone Interview with a homebound senior)

Heavenly Father: I bless you.

Homebound Senior: Lord, thank You. I'm calling You to sign up for work in Your Kingdom.

Heavenly Father: I see that you are willing to serve.

Homebound Senior: Yes, Lord, I am, but what can I do from my bed? I had an accident ten years ago and have been homebound ever since. I depend on others for all of my basic needs. And I am eighty years old.

Heavenly Father: Yes, I am well aware of your situation. And yes, I have an assignment for you.

Homebound Senior: You do? What is it?

Heavenly Father: You still have a good mind and you are resourceful. Use these strengths to encourage and to help others along the way to realize their goals. Use the media – television, telephone etc. – to build up those who come into your sphere of influence.

Homebound Senior: [Showing a bright smile] Yes, I can do that. I'll start right away. Thank You, Lord.

Heavenly Father: I love you. Now, go in peace and be a blessing to others.

The Tenacious Teacher

Heavenly Father: Daughter, are you here to serve in My Kingdom?

Ann: Yes, Lord, What do You want me to do?

Heavenly Father: I want you to teach My children in Sunday School.

Ann: Teach Sunday School? Teach children? Well ... Lord, I can't do that. You know how I'm living. I'm not fit to teach children.

Heavenly Father: Yes, I do know how you are living. Still, I want you to teach Sunday School.

Ann: Lord, don't You have a job cleaning the bathrooms or something like that. I'd rather work behind the scenes. You know that I want to obey You, but let me get my life together first, and then I'll do what You are saying.

Heavenly Father: Ann, I want to use you just the way you are.

Ann: Okay, help me to never make You ashamed, and I'll go.

Heavenly Father: Trust me. You are strong and able when you lean on me. I am your strength. I have given you everything you need to be a success. Teach and show children who I AM.

SKIT #5

THE PRISON CHAPLAIN

Heavenly Father: Welcome, daughter. Why are you here?

Mother: Lord, I'm here to answer Your call to service.

Heavenly Father: I'm looking for someone who will go into the prisons and tell of My delivering power, the power to soothe and comfort.

Mother: Oh, Lord, I am so afraid, but when do You want me to go?

Heavenly Father: I know that you're afraid, but I promise to be with you. Go now.

A mother of the church answered this call to serve and has served now for more than fifty years in prisons throughout the State of New York.

THE WILLING SOUL

Heavenly Father: Welcome, what brings you to this office today?

Angelo: I'm looking for a job. I was laid off from my engineering job of twenty years and have been looking for employment for the past two years.

Heavenly Father: What type of work are you looking for?

Angelo: I'll take whatever You have available.

Heavenly Father: You've come to the right place. The harvest is plentiful but the laborers are few. We have lots of work in many different areas. Are you willing to travel abroad?

Angelo: Yes Father, I am.

Heavenly Father: Son, pack your bags for India. I need you to use your skills to design and set up clean water systems for My people.

Angelo: Thank you, Lord, I will not disappoint You.

The Persevering Politician

Heavenly Father: Are you here to serve in My Kingdom?

Donald: Yes, I want to serve the people, to bring about equity and justice.

Heavenly Father: Will you be honest and courageous?

Donald: Yes, I will obey You, I will serve You, and I will honor You.

Heavenly Father: Will you look to Me for guidance and direction?

Donald: Yes, Lord, I will.

Heavenly Father: I've been waiting for you. Go, my son, serve in peace. You have chosen a worthy path.

"I
AM
THAT
I
AM"

Exodus 3:14, KJV

CHAPTER 4

GOD'S WORK AS REVEALED THROUGH HIS NAMES AND ACTIONS

I was very excited one day when I felt the Lord speak to me while I was sitting on the 85 bus on my way home from work. "Thank You, Lord," I prayed, "for answering my prayer about this book." He had suddenly showed me that His work is revealed in His many names. The thought actually came to me to try to write one chapter on each of God's names. What a massive undertaking that would have been! His names, however, do reveal what He does, for through them, His character is manifested every single day.

He is:

The Great I AM

El Shaddai   Lord God Almighty

El Elyon   The Most High God

Adonai   Lord, Master

Yahweh   Lord, Jehovah

Jehovah-Nissi   The Lord My Banner

Jehovah-Raah	The Lord My Shepherd
Jehovah-Rapha	The Lord That Heals
Jehovah-Shammah	The Lord Is There
Jehovah-Tsidkenu	The Lord Our Righteous
Jehovah-Mekoddishkem	The Lord Who Sanctifies You
El Olam	The Everlasting
Elohim	God
Qanna	Jealous
Jehovah-Jireh	The Lord Will Provide
Jehovah-Shalom	The Lord Is Peace
Jehovah-Sabaoth	The Lord of Hosts

No wonder I was so frustrated trying to write about His day! His works are far beyond our human comprehension.

GOD SPECIALZES IN MAKING THE IMPOSSIBLE POSSIBLE.

HE CAN DO WHAT NO OTHER POWER CAN DO.

Our God is the God of Action!

He Anoints: *"Thou anointest my head with oil; my cup runneth over"* (Psalm 23:5, KJV).

He Answers: *"Call to Me, and I will answer you, and show you great and mighty things which you do not know"* (Jeremiah 33:3).

He Blesses: *"Blessed are the peacemakers"* (Matthew 5:9).

He Cares: *"Casting all your care upon him, for he careth for you"* (1 Peter 5:7, KJV).

He Comforts: *"Blessed are those who mourn, for they shall be comforted"* (Matthew 5:4).

He Commands: *"Have I not commanded you? Be strong and of good courage; do not be afraid, nor be dismayed, for the Lord your God is with you wherever you go"* (Joshua 1:9).

He Creates: *"For by Him all things were created that are in heaven and that are on earth, visible and invisible"* (Colossians 1:16).

He Delights: *"For the Lord takes delight in His people; He crowns the humble with victory"* (Psalm 149:4).

He Delivers: *"The righteous cry out, and the LORD hears, and delivers them out of all their troubles"* (Psalm 34:17).

He Establishes: *"The LORD has established His throne in heaven, and His kingdom rules over all"* (Psalm 103:19).

He Executes: *"The LORD executeth righteousness and judgment for all that are oppressed"* (Psalm 103:6, KJV).

He Forgives: *"If we confess our sins, He is faithful and just to forgive us our sins and to cleanse us from all unrighteousness"* (1 John 1:9).

He Frees: *"Then you will know the truth, and the truth will set you free"* (John 8:32, CEB).

He Fulfills: *"He fulfills the desires of those who fear Him; He hears their cry and saves them"* (Psalm 145:19, NIV).

He Gathers: *"And he will send out his angels to gather his chosen ones from all over the world—from the farthest ends of the earth and heaven"* (Mark 13:27, NLT).

He Gives: *"Then my Father will give you whatever you ask for in my name"* (John 15:16, CEV).

He Heals: *"Jesus went throughout Galilee, teaching in their synagogues, preaching the good news of the king-*

dom, and healing every disease and sickness among the people" (Matthew 4:23, NIV).

He Hears: *"If my people, which are called by my name, shall humble themselves, and pray, and seek my face, and turn from their wicked ways; then I will hear from heaven, and forgive their sin, and will heal their land"* (2 Chronicles 7:14, KJV).

He Helps: *"Now go; I will help you speak and will teach you what to say"* (Exodus 4:12, NIV).

He Increases: *"He gives strength to the weary and increases the power of the weak"* (Isaiah 40:29, NIV).

He Judges: *"It is God who judges: He brings one down, He exalts another"* (Psalm 75:7, NIV).

He Keeps: *"You will keep him in perfect peace, whose mind is stayed on You, because he trusts in You"* (Isaiah 26:3).

He Longs: *"Yet the LORD longs to be gracious to you; therefore He will rise up to show you compassion. For the LORD is a God of justice. Blessed are all who wait for Him!"* (Isaiah 30:18, NIV).

He Looks: *"But Jesus looked at them and said to them, 'With men this is impossible, but with God all things are possible' "* (Matthew 19:26).

He Loves: *"For God so loved the world, that He gave His only begotten Son, that whoever believes in Him should not perish but have everlasting life"* (John 3:16).

He Moves: *"And the Spirit of God moved upon the face of the waters"* (Genesis 1:2, KJV).

He Numbers: *"He determines the number of the stars and calls them each by name"* (Psalm 147:4, NIV).

He Observes: *"He rules by His power forever; His eyes observe the nations"* (Psalm 66:7).

He Plans: *" 'For I know the plans I have for you,' declares the LORD, 'plans to prosper you and not to harm you, plans to give you hope and a future' "* (Jeremiah 29:11, NIV).

He Preserves: *"The Lord protects and preserves them—they are counted among the blessed in the land—he does not give them over to the desire of their foes"* (Psalm 41:2, NIV).

He Provides: *"God is faithful, and he will not let you be tempted beyond your ability, but with the temptation he will also provide the way of escape, that you may be able to endure it"* (1 Corinthians 10:13, ESV).

He Qualifies: *"It is not that we think we are qualified to do anything on our own. Our qualification comes from God"* (2 Corinthians 3:5, NLT).

He Reigns: *"The Lord reigns; let the earth rejoice; let the multitude of isles be glad"* (Psalm 97:1)!

He Remembers: *"He remembers His covenant forever, the promise He made for a thousand generations"* (Psalm 105:8, NIV).

He Rescues: *"Rescue me from my enemies, L*ORD*, for I hide myself in you"* (Psalm 143:9, NIV).

He Rewards: *"Whatever you do, work at it with all your heart, as working for the Lord, not for men, since you know that you will receive an inheritance from the Lord as a reward, It is the Lord Christ you are serving"* (Colossians 3:23-24, NIV).

He Rules: *"For the kingdom is the L*ORD*'s, and He rules over the nations"* (Psalm 22:28).

He Sanctifies: *"Sanctify them by the truth; your word is truth"* (John 17:17, NIV).

He Saves: *"For the Son of man is come to seek and to save that which was lost"* (Luke 19:10, KJV).

He Searches: *"I, the L*ORD*, search the heart; I test the mind"* (Jeremiah 17:10).

He Sends: *"Also I heard the voice of the L*ORD*, saying, Whom shall I send and who will go for us? Then said I, Here am I; send me"* (Isaiah 6:8, KJV).

He Speaks: *"But when they arrest you, do not worry about what to say or how to say it. At that time you will be given what to say, for it will not be you speaking, but the Spirit of your Father speaking through you"* (Matthew 10:19-20, NIV).

He Strengthens: *"I can do all things through Christ, who strengthens me"* (Philippians 4:13).

He Supplies: *"But my God shall supply all your needs according to his riches in glory by Christ Jesus"* (Philippians 4:19, KJV).

He Teaches: *"Jesus said, 'If you hold to my teaching, you are really my disciples' "* (John 8:31, NIV).

He Thinks: *"As the heavens are higher than the earth, so are My ways higher than your ways and My thoughts than your thoughts"* (Isaiah 55:9, NIV).

He Understands: *"He made their hearts, so he understands everything they do"* (Psalm 33:15, NLT).

He Values: *"Fear ye not therefore, ye are of more value than many sparrows"* (Matthew 10:31, KJV).

He Waits: *"Therefore, the LORD will wait, that He may be gracious to you and therefore He will be exalted"* (Isaiah 30:18).

He Watches: *"I am watching to see that my word is fulfilled"* (Jeremiah 1:12, NIV).

He Wipes: *"He will wipe every tear from their eyes"* (Revelation 21:4, NIV).

He Works: *"And we know that in all things God works for the good of those who love him, who have been called according to his purpose"* (Romans 8:28, NIV).

Wow! He is a mighty God!

"**I AM**
ALPHA and **OMEGA,**
the beginning and the end,
the first and the last."

Revelation 22:13 KJV

Chapter 5

God's Work of Answering Our Prayers

Oh, the joy of being in the presence of the Lord! In His presence, there is fullness of joy:

You will show me the path of life;
In Your presence is fullness of joy;
At Your right hand are pleasures forevermore.

Psalm 16:11

Jesus is welcoming our presence to come to Him in prayer and present our needs to Him, to be free in prayer, to be real, to tell Him all about it, to tell Him how much we love Him, to tell Him what are the concerns of our hearts. One of my most common prayers is this: "Oh, Lord, how we need You every single day, day by day!"

In the presence of the Lord there is peace and comfort, knowing that He cares for us and that He is in control, even when we feel out of control. In His presence, I can be secure and know that He hears me. He can deal with my good, bad and ugly. He can fix me. One of our most important prayers should be, "Lord, help me to forgive those who have hurt me."

But in prayer, we can ask whatever we happen to need at the moment:

And whatever things you ask in prayer, believing, you will receive.   Matthew 21:22

Let them give thanks to the LORD for his unfailing love and his wonderful deeds for men.   Psalm 107:15, NIV

Sing to him, sing praise to him; tell of all his wonderful acts.   Psalm 105:2, NIV

What a wonderful comfort this is to know!

GOD DELIVERS US:

God is our Deliverer in today's world. He is still performing signs, wonders and miracles. Here are some of the things He does in any given day, as reported by the media:

A Mountain Lion Attack

April 30, 1998 near Englewood, Colorado — Andy Peterson survived a terrifying mountain lion attack in Roxborough State Park. As a result, Lion King Ministries was founded, and Andy continues to share his testimony of God's grace and mercy to people all around the world.

A Miraculous Water Rescue

2006, Pueblo, Colorado – Charlene Deherrera was rescued from a submerged SUV that sank in ten feet of water. All four windows were still closed when her vehicle was brought to the surface. No one could explain how her vehicle was opened enough to get her out and then closed again.

A Window Washer In a Coma Woke Up on Christmas Day

January 2008 – Alcides Moreno was washing windows when he fell forty-seven stories from a Manhattan skyscraper. He woke up from his coma on Christmas day.

La Miracilee (The Miracle Girl)

June 30, 2009 – Bahia Bakari, a thirteen-year-old French girl was the sole survivor of Yemenia Flight 626, a major airplane crash into the Indian Ocean near the north coast of Grande Comore, Comoros. She clung to a piece of plane wreckage for more than nine hours without a life vest, mostly in pitch darkness, before being rescued. All of the other 152 passengers were killed, including her mother.

Buried for 27 days: Haiti Earthquake Survivor

March 28, 2010, Port de Prince, Haiti – Evans Monsignac is thought to be the longest earthquake survivor. He was rescued from the debris after 27 days. His survival has confounded doctors and defies medical logic. In his own words, "I was resigned to death, but God gave me life. The fact that I'm alive today isn't because of me. It is because of the grace of God. It's a miracle. I can't explain it."

Boy Falls 16 Floors and Lives

July 26, 2010 Manukau City, Auckland – A 15-year-old boy survived a 16-story fall and lived. Medical experts were amazed that he was not killed.

Miners Trapped Underground in Chile

August 5, 2010 — Chilean miners were lifted to safety after being trapped underground for 69 days.

A Baby Survives an Earthquake

March 14, 2011, Ishiniomaki, Japan — After an earthquake and tsunami, a four-month-old baby was pulled from the debris. She was dressed in a pink woolen bear suit.

A Baby Buried Alive in Turkey

October 25, 2011 — A two-week-old baby was rescued alive from a building destroyed in an earthquake.

A Six-Year-Old Rescued

November 25, 2012, Vermont U.S.A – JoJo McCray was rescued after he was separated from his family in the woods. He survived twenty hours of freezing weather without a cellphone or radio.

A Woman Trapped in a Wrecked Car

August, 7, 2013, Missouri, USA – A woman, Kate Lentz, was trapped in a car after being hit head-on by a drunk driver. She asked the rescue workers to pray outloud. An unidentified priest showed up and anointed the car with oil. He then told the rescuers that they would be able to free her from the car, and they did. When they turned around to thank the priest, he was nowhere to be found – even though the roads were all blocked off.

A Thanksgiving Miracle

November 26, 2014, Newburgh, New York — Two New York boys, ages 9 and 11, were rescued alive after being buried and trapped under several feet of snow for more than 4 hours in 20 degree weather. The boys were building a snow fort when a plow accidentally piled more snow on top of them.

Alaska Man Survives Three Days Lost in Sub-Zero Temps, Fights Off Wolverine

December 15, 2014, Alaska, USA — Craig Johnson says "I think it's a miracle that I'm alive." He survived three days in below-zero temperatures, and a wolverine following him. He walked 30 miles searching for help. He used warning shots and a stick to defend himself against the animal. Mr.

Johnson was finally rescued by his cousin, who heard his yells for help.

Seven-Year-Old Girl Is Sole Survivor in Kentucky Plane Crash

January 3, 2015 – The bruised child pulled herself out of the upside-down wreckage and walked through a wooded area to the home of a stranger to get help. Her mother, father, sister and cousin were killed in the crash.

Driver's Miracle Escape from a Crashed Car in Germany

September 21, 2015 – A high-speed racing car hit a barrier, bounced in the air and rolled down the track at Nurburgring race track in Germany. The driver walked away unharmed.

God Heals Us:

My Testimony – An Emotional Healing

Sometimes we are busy helping others and don't realize that we need healing ourselves. It happened to me. On October 7, 2013, I wrote the following:

I remember as a child that we had a rhyme that went something like this: "Rich man, Poor man, Beggar man, Thief, Doctor, Lawyer, Indian Chief." As we sang that rhyme, while jumping double dutch, we never wanted the rope to collapse on "poor man," "beggar man" or "thief." If it did, we would shout "Do Over! Do Over!" Somehow we instinctively knew enough to resist such a low status in life.

I would sometimes wonder what I was going to be when I grew up. I often had dreams of being a nun (yes, me, a nun), because I liked helping other people. I was always the teacher when we played school and the mother when we played house.

My parents were southerners and well acquainted with the limitations placed on people of color during that time. They strove to give us — their children — a part of the American Dream.

During my elementary school years, we lived in the Farragut Housing Projects in Brooklyn, New York. When I reached the 5th grade, my parents and school officials decided to "bus" me and one of my brothers to a school in the predominately white, upper class, Prospect Park section of Brooklyn. That year we kids who rode our bus, all from the housing projects, pretty much stayed to ourselves.

Promotion to the 6th grade proved to be a painful experience for me, as I was one of only three "Negroes" in my 6th-grade class and was often subjected to teasing, rejection and misunderstanding.

The other problem was that this was culture shock for me. The way my classmates dressed, the jewelry they wore, and the money they had for lunch was so different from the world I was accustomed to.

I think the worst part of all was feeling like an "outcast," especially when no one wanted to hold my hand as we lined up two-by-two for the walk to our classroom from the schoolyard. And I was also almost always the last one to be picked for team play and contests.

My saving grace at that school was Mr. "D." He was my 5th-grade teacher, a white man, I believe Italian. Mr. D. was very sensitive and supportive of what I was going through. Sometimes he would find me crying in the hallway. He would say, "Linda, you're smart, and you're just as good as they are." These pep talks helped me through that difficult year.

Eventually I took and passed an advanced academic test and, as a result, was seldom the last one to be chosen for the spelling bee teams. However, at the end of the 6th grade, I vowed never to return to that school. I went on to enjoy a reasonable measure of success, believing that I had overcome the experience.

After feeling the need to write this book, I joined an on-line writing course. We were given seven subjects that we had to write something on. Upon receiving "The Wounded Healer" Archetype as my assignment, I decided to write about my busing challenge, believing that I had overcome it all. I was wrong. As I wrote I found that the memories of those days were still raw, painfully uncomfortable and moved me to tears. It was obvious that I was not yet healed, so I determined that it was time to face this giant, time to forgive, time to take action and heal.

On September 26, 2013, I boarded the "F" train to the Prospect Park Station and then took Bus 68 to 11th Avenue. Walking toward the school gave me an adrenalin rush. As I looked around, it seemed as if time had stood still. Everything looked exactly the same.

Boldly approaching, with anxious anticipation of my freedom from the sludge of fifty years of unforgiveness, I walked around the school. Focusing on the playground, I noticed there were minority staff and grinned as I looked at the flagpole, reminiscing about the Maypole ceremony we had performed those two years.

I went inside to inquire about the teachers and principal who used to be there and found that none of them were still there. Then I felt that the moment had arrived. Outside again, looking upward, I placed my hands on the fence in front of the school and, as the faces of those who hurt me appeared, I genuinely forgave each and every one of them. I said a prayer of thanksgiving to God, blew three kisses of goodwill toward my school of hard knocks and walked away smiling. I was relieved. I was free. I was a wounded healer.

Dear reader, why not dedicate yourself to be an agent of God's love? As a beginning, hastily forgive those who have hurt you. In this way, you, too, can be healed by God's love.

A Physical, Emotional, Mental, and Spiritual Healing

My name is Steve. Sometimes, in the world of addiction, God ceases to exist to the user. While suffering with the addiction of alcohol, I also used marijuana and cocaine, I stopped calling on God to help get me out of the situation, because the moment I felt better I went back to repeating the behavior, swearing that I would not do it again.

As my addiction progressed, I blamed God for being in this situation since I no longer had anyone else to blame. After all, He was God, and He could do anything, so why didn't He help me get out of that situation? I stopped believing in Him.

I suffered with pancreatitis, liver damage, convulsions, dehydration and other medical conditions. My emotional and mental state was one of confusion, and eventually I became homeless. Then one day I found myself lying in a bed in a detox ward, restrained and disoriented. To this day I have no knowledge of how I got there and later how I wound up in a VA Rehabilitation Center in upstate New York.

Through all of this, God humbled me in spite of myself and directed me to Alcoholics Anonymous, where people like myself were getting help. I later discovered, after hearing the poem "Footprints," that it had been God who carried me throughout my insane ordeal.

It was only by the grace of God that I stopped using alcohol and other drugs and by His grace that I was delivered. He healed my mind, body and spirit, and I have long since accepted Him back as my Lord and Savior!

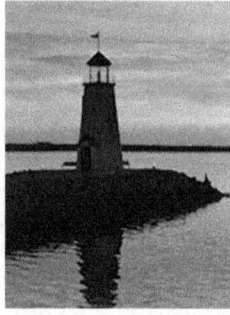

CHAPTER 6

GOD'S WORK OF POURING OUT HIS LOVE

September 10, 2013: I got up in the morning with the Lord on my mind. "Love, love, love ... ," I heard Him say. "Tell My people about My love." I read the entire book of First Corinthians. What a blessing! Oh, God, Your love is awesome!

December 31, 2013: I got up this morning because of God's love, mercy and grace. As I was riding my exercise bike in my office, I contemplated, "How can I write about God's day without knowing His mind, the mind of Christ? Can I know what is on the mind of Christ? Surely that would govern His actions." Suddenly I had a desire to know more about the mind of Christ.

Despite several distractions, I finally googled for supporting scriptures on the mind of Christ, and here's what I found:

Romans 12:2, RSV

Do not be conformed to this world, but be transformed by the renewal of your mind, that by testing you may discern what is the will of God, what is good and acceptable and perfect.

Philippians 2:5, RSV

Have this mind among yourselves, which is yours in Christ Jesus.

1 John 2:6, AMP

Whoever says he abides in him ought to walk in the same way in which he walked.

Ephesians 5:1, RSV

Therefore be imitators of God, as beloved children.

One thing was certain. The heart of God is full of love and He desires our worship, praise and adoration, to show that we love Him too. The mind of God is to do His will. We must learn to take the concerns of God's people to Him in prayer.

My thoughts roamed from prayer, fasting and the Holy Spirit back to the love of our Creator and King. He is so merciful and tender, our greatest Comforter.

I felt compelled to go and tell of His sacrifice and His love for us, a love that still abides, a love that saves, heals, delivers, comforts every day and is manifested in the lives of His people on a second-by-second basis. Now was that an answer or what?

On August 8, 2013, I went to the library and got some books on writing. The problem must be with my writing skills. I would have to learn more to accomplish this task. All the while I kept thinking: God is a God of love. Talk about the love of God.

On the morning of Tuesday, October 1, 2013, I again sought the Lord about this message. I was stuck again. I had meant to continue the night before, after having spent about three hours rearranging the office to make it more conducive to writing, but then I wasn't able to continue. What was I missing?

I had come downstairs at about 4:00 in the morning. I listened to praise and worship music and then reached for the Word. I opened the Bible at John 17, Jesus' prayer to the heavenly Father before being betrayed. I read the prayer three times, seeing things I had never seen before. God loves us just like He loves His Son. Wow! I had to get down on my knees with that thought. Oh, what love!

CHARACTERISTICS OF LOVE FROM 2 CORINTHIANS 13:4-8:

- Love is patient.
- Love is kind.
- Love does not envy.
- Love does not boast.
- Love is not proud.
- Love is not rude.
- Love is not self-seeking.
- Love is not easily angered.
- Love keeps no record of wrongs.
- Love does not delight in evil but, rather, rejoices with

the truth.
- Love always protects.
- Love always trusts.
- Love always hopes.
- Love always perseveres.
- Love never fails

It is God's very nature to love:

- The love of God (*agape* in Greek) is very different from what the world calls "love." There is no comparison.
- Everything that God does is motivated by love because He is love.
- His love is intentional and of His own choosing.
- His love in unconditional and eternal.
- The love of God is what created and sustains all of creation.
- His love is unconditional and is not predicated upon our deeds, for the Bible states that even our righteousness is like filthy rags.
- His love is manifested in all of His creation.
- We can depend on His love.
- The love of God supersedes anything that we could ever think or imagine.
- His love is tangible,
- His love is overwhelming.
- We have no way to measure His love in human terms.
- His love is patient, kind and enduring.

- He loves us even when we mess up.
- His love is strong.
- His love is our anchor.
- His love is our constant companion.
- He declares His love and glory in the earth every single day.

What God's Love Does:

- His love is our guide
- His loves corrects us.
- His love gives us hope.
- His love takes care of us.
- His love frees us, and breaks our chains of bondage.
- His love gives us strength.
- His love looks for the best in us.
- His love helps us to put one foot in front of the other.
- His love beckons us to Him.
- His love is comprehensive and meets our deepest needs: identify, security, acceptance and purpose.
- His love lifts us from the muck and the mire of sin.
- His love is redemptive.
- His love is our moral compass.
- His love humbles us
- His love helps us through our trials, tribulations and suffering.

God is a spirit and those who worship Him must worship Him in spirit and in truth (see John 4:23).

To know Him is to love Him, and to love Him is to serve Him.

God's love is beautifully expressed in the most beloved verse of the Bible:

John 3:16

For God so loved the world, that He gave His only be-gotten son, that whosoever believes in Him, will have everlasting life.

One thing is certain: The heart of God is full of love, and He desires our worship, praise and adoration, to show that we love Him too.

GOD IS LOVE

BY

KATHERINE SCOTT McIVER

For God so LOVED the world that He gave His only begotten Son, that whoever believes in Him should not perish but have everlasting life. John 3:16

What is love? Whether we know it or not, **LOVE** comes from GOD, for **LOVE IS GOD**. Ask a random sampling of men, women, boys and girls of varying ages and at different seasons of their lives to define love, and you will get an array of responses, most of them based on emotions.

Humans, created just below the angels, experience different kinds of love within a given day and certainly during a lifetime. Still, we find it difficult to explain or define what love really is. Therefore we use three Greek words — *philia*, *storge*, and *eros* — to shed light on the degrees and depth of emotions we humans feel for each other.

Philia is often described as brotherly love or friendship. It translates into the warm feelings we have for our friends. There is a fondness we feel toward those with whom we share common interests.

The special bond or natural love parents have for their children and children for their parents and family for family is termed *storge*. These two words are interestingly combined in Romans 12:10 where followers of Christ, children of God, are instructed: *"Be kindly affectionate to one another with brotherly love, in honor giving preference to one another."*

Another type of love is *eros.* This is the sensual and sexual love, created by God for the purpose of bringing two individuals together physically, which may or may not result in reproduction. More often than not, humans have the tendency to set up conditions or limits to determine if they will give and receive love.

We Christians use the word *agape* to speak of the ultimate love experience, God's love for us. Those who have a relationship with Christ know that God is Love and His love is selfless and unconditional.

Throughout the Scriptures, time and time again, we see the forgiveness of God toward His children. That's just Who He is. Everything about our Father is LOVE. Some have not yet come to the realization of God's love and, unfortunately, others have chosen to totally reject this good and perfect gift from the One who loves us all still.

How does God pour out His love on us? He brings needed sleep to tired bodies and wakes us up to brand new mornings, new beginnings, dreams we haven't imagined, and to love we continue to experience. He grants us desired answers to prayers. Even when we don't get what we ask for, we still see and feel His love, because He equips us with peace and the strength to go through whatever we are facing at the moment. He clothes us with spiritual armor to emerge from the battles of life victoriously. It is amazing how, looking back over our trials, the focus is not on the trials but, rather, on how God carried us through those valleys. This makes us to know that He loves us.

One family can say: "He has put food on our table and clothes on our backs, opened doors for us to successful careers and provided us with comfortable and safe shelter. There are no illnesses that He has not cured. There have been times of sorrow; that is to be expected. But hard times never last long. He is our Shepherd. He loves us, and we love Him."

Another family is homeless, sleeping wherever they can find a place to come in out of the heat or cold. Thanksgiving, Christmas and Easter are times they anxiously await, but not so much because of the religious or spiritual meanings they represent. It is because of the economic support the family receives from the organizations sponsoring the events. They have been living like this, off and on, for many years. More on than off. They also declare: "He is our Shepherd. He loves us, and we love Him."

How is it that one life seems to be sailing along almost effortlessly, generation after generation, and the other one is constantly under attack, taking on deeper roots day after day, month after month, and year after year? Still, each one claims God as the One who guides and loves them. How can such dramatically different life experiences bring each one to the same conclusion, the same truth, that He is their Shepherd Who loves unconditionally? Perhaps somewhere during the course of their lives their spiritual ears were opened long enough to hear about God and Jesus, and their hearts were also opened to accept the truth of the infinite "I AM."

Every day we continue to do something, by thought or action, that is not pleasing to our Father. We may see that something as big or small. God calls it sin and therefore punishment by death is in order. However, God viewed man's past, present and future, saw sin and decided that a sinless person would have to take the nails and crown of thorns for man. Paul states, in **Romans 5:8, *"But God shows his love for us in that while we were yet sinners, Christ died for us"* (RSV). In 1 John 4:9-11 we read, *"In this the love of God was manifested toward us, that God has sent His only begotten Son into the world, that we might live through Him. In this is love, not that we loved God, but that He loved us and sent His Son to be the propitiation for our sins. Beloved, if God so loved us, we also ought to love one another."***

Christ would pay the price once for our past, present and future deeds. At the cross and the empty tomb, love was profoundly demonstrated. Again John reemphases this fact when he writes, *"By this we know love, because He laid down His life for us. And we also ought to lay down our lives for the brethren"* (1 John 3:16).

From the beginning, God's plan was to love us, and that has not changed. Nor will it change. We only have to digest the promise and bask in this assurance of God's love:

Who shall separate us from the love of Christ? Shall tribulation, or distress, or persecution, or famine, or nakedness, or peril or sword? As it is written:

"For Your sake we are killed all day long;
We are accounted as sheep for the slaughter."

Yet in all these things we are more than conquerors through Him who loved us. For I am persuaded that neither death nor life, nor angels nor principalities nor powers, nor things present nor things to come, nor height nor depth, nor any other created thing shall be able to separate us from the love of God which is in Christ Jesus our Lord.

Romans 8:35-39

One of the main lessons small children learn in Sunday School and one that stays with them throughout life is found in the sweet song, *Jesus Loves Me; This I Know.* Later in life, we sometimes tend to lose sight of that truth. Let us remember to go back in time, take on the eyes, ears and heart of a child again and know that God truly loves us. He is pouring out His love on us every second of every day because that is His character. God is the Creator of love! *God is love!*

CHAPTER 7

GOD'S WORK OF BRINGING US TO PRAISE

Oh that men would praise the LORD for his goodness, and for his wonderful works to the children of men!

Psalm 107:15

Tell of all his wondrous works!   Psalm 105:2, ESV

On December 30, 2011, I was led to write down scriptures that encourage us to praise God for how He cares for us each day:

1 Peter 5:7, ESV

Casting all your anxieties on him, because he cares for you.

Proverbs 1:33, NIV

But whoever listens to me will live in safety and be at ease, without fear of harm.

Psalm 8:4-6, KJV

What is man that You are mindful of him,
And the son of man that You visit him?
For You have made him a little lower than the angels,
And You have crowned him with glory and honor.
You have made him to have dominion over the works
of Your hands;
You have put all things under his feet.

Psalm 23:1

The Lord is my shepherd;
I shall not want.

Luke 12:7

Indeed the very hairs of your head are all numbered.
Do not fear; you are more valuable than many sparrows.

Jeremiah 29:11

"For I know the plans I have for you," says the LORD,
"They are plans for good and not for disaster, to give
you a future and a hope."
For I know the thoughts that I think toward you, saith
the LORD, thoughts of peace, and not of evil, to give
you an expected end. (KJV)

Isaiah 41:10, NIV

"So do not fear, for I am with you; do not be dismayed,
for I am your God. I will strengthen you and help you;
I will uphold you with my right hand"

Matthew 11:28-29

*Come to me, all you who are weary and burdened, and
I will give you rest. Take my yoke upon you and learn
from me, for I am gentle and humble in heart, and you
will find rest for your souls.*

Psalm 91:11, ESV

*For he will command his angels concerning you to
guard you in all your ways.*

Hebrews 2:8-9, KJV

*Thou hast put all things in subjection under his feet.
For in that he put all in subjection under him, he left
nothing that is not put under him. But now we see not
yet all things put under him. But we see Jesus, who
was made a little lower than the angels for the suffering of death, crowned with glory and honour; that he
by the grace of God should taste death for every man.*

What awesome love!

It's Personal

The question is: How do you know that God cares for
you? Some would answer in this way:

- I know God cares because of the love, kindness
  and blessings that He gives me, my children and my
  grandchildren every single day.

- I cried out to God for money to feed my children. He caused the wind to blow a $20 bill right to me, and with that I was able to purchase enough groceries for a whole week.
- God sent a doctor to perform my surgery for free when I did not have money to pay.
- The Lord kept my mind when I was on the verge of losing it.
- God comforted me and took away the terrible pain I experienced with the death of my son.
- God brought me out of ten years of incarceration. Now that's caring. I know He cares for me.
- In my night season, He dried my tears, showing me how much He cares.
- When I thought I was going blind and all hope was gone, He restored my sight.
- As a new teacher, I was nervous about teaching and needed a lot of help. I prayed to God, and He showed me how to setup the room, arrange the seating of the students and how to present my lesson.
- I was sick and needed to travel to another state for medical attention. God sent someone to purchase my airfare and another person I had only met twice to cover me in prayer.
- God heard my prayers, and I was accepted by the college of my choice.
- My daughter was accepted by a prestigious high school, and I had no money to purchase her ward-

robe. God showed me how to be creative and make clothes for her — even though I had never taken a single sewing lesson.

Answers from our Youth

- I know God cares because He delivers me out of my situations.
- God cares for me because He sacrificed His life for me.
- God loves me, and I love God.
- God cares for me because He gives me food and clothes.
- My teacher told me that I was going to be held back in the third grade if I did not get better grades. I prayed to God and asked Him to help me get good grades. I did my work, and I got As and Bs and was promoted to the fourth grade.
- There were some boys in my school who were doing bad things. I asked God to help me not to be like them, but to do the right thing. The result was that I did not get into trouble.
- I was walking across the street when a paper I was holding fell out of my hand. I bent down to pick it up and suddenly a car came speeding out of nowhere and missed running over me by a few inches. I know God cares for me. He saved my life.
- I thank God for my mother and father.
- Because I'm going to see my father on Friday.

- Because He helped me pass my test in school.
- Because He gave me a little brother to play with.
- Jesus is my Savior. He sacrificed His life for me.

CHAPTER 8

My Conclusion

So what was my conclusion about this entire matter? One evening I found that my mind was about to explode with it all. Who can comprehend God's greatness? Who can measure His love? I used to hear my elders saying: "He is so high, you can't get over Him, so low you can't get under Him, and so wide you can't get around Him. He is God, and God, all by Himself, is completely self-sufficient." I realized again how much I depended on Him, and I could only say, "How Great Thou Art!"

I repented. Why should I complain about anything? God had taken care of me all day long. He had included me in His plan. He saw to it that my strength didn't give out. Most wonderful of all, I was able to talk to Him about my day. He was always available. He was never too busy, and He loved me.

I realized that I needed to get proper rest and take better care of myself. I needed to seek Him first in all things. I needed to put Him first in the morning. I needed to be obedient to everything He showed me. There is something about doing things God's way that preserves us. Instead of rushing home to see the evening news, I would rush home to spend time with Him, seeking His face for direction and guidance.

And as I prayed, I was energized. How could I not praise Him for His power, might, wisdom and knowledge! He is all-powerful, all knowledge (all-knowing) and all love. And He is in control. My God is a Mind-Blower. He is the Creator, Sustainer and Maintainer of the entire Universe.

An Invitation To Christ

Jesus said to him, "I am the way, the truth, and the life. No one comes to the Father except through Me."

John 14:6

Paul wrote to the Romans:

If you confess with your mouth the Lord Jesus and believe in your heart that God has raised Him from the dead, you will be saved. For with the heart one believes unto righteousness, and with the mouth confession is made unto salvation.   Romans 10:9-10

Here's how you can receive Christ as your Lord and Savior right this moment:

- Admit that you are a sinner (see Romans 3:20).
- Repent (turn from sin) (see Acts 17:30).
- Believe that Jesus Christ died for you, was buried and rose from the dead (see Romans 10:9-10).
- Invite Jesus into your life, to become your personal Savior (see Romans 10:13).

If you don't know what to pray, you might want to say a prayer like this:

Dear God,

I am a sinner. Forgive me of my sin. I believe that Jesus Christ shed His precious blood and died to save me. I now invite Christ to come into my heart and life as my personal Savior.

Amen!

If you prayed that prayer, then welcome into the family of God. You are now a new creature in Christ:

Therefore, if anyone is in Christ, he is a new creation; old things have passed away; behold, all things have become new. 2 Corinthians 5:17

Ask God to lead you to a church where Christ is preached and the Bible (the Word of God) is the highest and final authority. Be faithful to that church so that you can grow in grace and develop the special talents and abilities God has placed within you. And be sure to seek your special place of service in God's Kingdom. He has something unique and exciting for you to do for Him.

DIVINE INSPIRATIONS MESSENGER

AUTHOR CONTACT PAGE

You may reach the author at the following addresses:

Linda Gourdine-Hunt
Divine Inspirations Messenger

email: lindaagh3@aol.com
Lindahunt26@gmail.com

www.vacanciesinthekingdomofgod.com
www.thepublishedword.com

Other Books by Linda Gourdine-Hunt

Help Wanted! Vacancies in the Kingdom of God is a call to action for those who are unsure or need direction on how to serve God in His Kingdom.

* Available also as a Kindle book.

Oportunidades de empleo is the Spanish version.

* Available also as a Kindle book.

What Shall I Render?

My Prayer Requests

_____

_____

_____

_____

_____

_____

_____

_____

_____

_____

_____

_____

_____

_____

_____

_____

_____

_____

_____

_____

_____

_____

_____

My Prayer Requests

_____
_____
_____
_____
_____
_____
_____
_____
_____
_____
_____
_____
_____
_____
_____
_____
_____
_____
_____
_____
_____
_____
_____
_____

Answered Prayers

Answered Prayers

www.ingramcontent.com/pod-product-compliance
Lightning Source LLC
Chambersburg PA
CBHW031605040426
42452CB00006B/419